EASTER
Program Builder No. 32

Compiled by
Kim Messer

Questions? Please write or call:

Lillenas Publishing Company
Drama Resources
P. O. Box 419527
Kansas City, MO 64141
Phone: 816-931-1900 • Fax: 816-412-8390
E-mail: drama@lillenas.com
Web Site: www.lillenasdrama.com

Cover Design: Rick Day
Interior Design: Sharon Page
Executive Editor: Kim Messer
Copy Editor: Kimberly Meiste
Manuscript Formatting: Karen Phillips

Contents

Preschool Recitations

Easter to Me

Here's what Easter is to me,
Jesus came to set us free!
Thank You, God, for what You've
done
Through Your one and only Son.

Ray Ressem

Candy

Easter candy is sweet,
But Jesus can't be beat!
He's alive and in my heart.
He has known me from the start!

Susan Harrison

Upon the Cross

CHILD 1: Jesus there upon the cross,
CHILD 2: Dying so we are not lost.
CHILD 3: What's amazing? Can't
you see?
CHILD 4: He did it just for you
and me.

Ray Ressem

Jesus Is Awesome!

Jesus is awesome, can't you see?
He loves you and He loves me.
He rose again on Easter day.
He **really** is the only way!

Susan Harrison

What Would Be?

CHILD 1: On the cross all seemed
lost.
CHILD 2: Jesus died. The people
cried.
CHILD 3: On day three, what
would be?
ALL: Empty grave! Jesus saves!

Ray Ressem

See the Cross

(Have children create a large picture of a cross and a large picture of an empty tomb. As the children say this short rhyme, they show the pictures to the audience.)

See the cross? *(Show the cross picture)*
Such sad loss.
See the grave? *(Show the empty tomb
picture)*
Jesus saves!

Ray Ressem

Weak

He made himself weak,
Even though so strong.
He gave up all
And had done no wrong.

Susan Harrison

Wow, God, Wow

Wow, God, wow.
You did it somehow,

Sent Your Son to die.
Now we get to fly
With You way up high,
Heaven in the sky.

Wow, God, wow.
You did it somehow.

Ray Ressem

Recitations for Ages 5 to 7

What Easter Is For

Easter is a time for family and
friends;
For good food that never seems
to end.
For egg hunts, chocolate, and so
much more.
But remember what Easter is for—
It is about Christ, the risen Lord.

Susan Harrison

I Like Easter

I like Easter.
I like the bunnies and the chocolate
and the cards.
I like Easter.
It's a fun, fun time.
I like Easter.
I like how God gave His life for you
and me!

Traci and Ethan Matt

A Joyous Easter

Jesus overcame the grave
And rose to *life anew*.
When we believe in Jesus' love
We receive a *new life* too!

Dorothy Heibel

Have You Met Him?

Have you met my Friend?
His name is Jesus and His love will
never end.
He died for me and for you too,
And in heaven with Him, you'll
never be blue!

Susan Harrison

Recitations for Ages 8 to 10

The Cross

(Each CHILD *holds a cross or picture of a cross that they made as they recite their line.)*

CHILD 1: The Cross . . . it is more than jewelry.

CHILD 2: The Cross . . . it is where Jesus gave His life.

CHILD 3: The Cross . . . it is powerful when you believe it.

CHILD 4: The Cross . . . it represents the One who can give you life.

CHILD 5: The Cross . . . you only need to accept.

Susan Harrison

Sleeping In

The weekend was jam-packed with family and friends
And the holiday rush seemed to go without end.
At bedtime my dad said, "I'm worn pretty thin.
How 'bout in the morning we plan to sleep in."

"You've got to be kidding," I said in dismay.
"Tomorrow is not just another Lord's Day.
Tomorrow's the day we remember the gloom
That was lifted when Jesus walked out of the tomb.
We remember the way He beat Satan real bad,
And we think of the joy that His followers had."

"Why, you're right," said my mom.
"Way to go," said my dad.
And it turned out to be the best Easter we'd had.

Traci Matt

He Did It for You and Me

(Perform with two children. The first one recites to the audience while the second one looks at the first CHILD.*)*

CHILD 1: They hurt Him.
CHILD 2: *He did it for you and me.*
CHILD 1: They made fun of Him.
CHILD 2: *He did it for you and me.*
CHILD 1: Our sins were on Him.
CHILD 2: *He did it for you and me.*
CHILD 1: He was killed.
CHILD 2: *He did it for you and me.*
CHILD 1: He was buried.
CHILD 2: *He did it for you and me.*
CHILD 1: He rose again!
CHILD 2: *He did it for you and me!*
BOTH: We have eternal life because
He did it for you and me!

Susan Harrison

Youth and Adult Recitations

Flower Song

(May be used with one or two readers.)

Tulips dancing in yellow and red
    Remind us of the words He said,
"I have come to give you life."

Daffodils dipping in the breeze
    Remind us of Jesus on His knees,
"Let this cup pass from me."

Crocuses peeking from beneath the snow
    Remind us that the world must know,
"No one comes to the Father but by Me."

Daisies smiling in fields without end
    Remind us of a home with our friend.
"I go to prepare a place for you."

Traci Matt

Who Is Christ?

Christ . . . God's Son.
Christ . . . God.
Christ . . . the Lamb.
Christ . . . the Redeemer.
Christ . . . the Savior.

What does it all mean? Knowing and believing are two separate things.
Know and you have information, believe and you will be saved.
The Bible is true, every word. Come to Him. He is ready to accept you.

Susan Harrison

Cross Colors

The cross draped in purple speaks of a King.
  One of a servant whose praises we sing.
The cross draped in black speaks of our grief
  For the One who was murdered alongside a thief.
The cross draped in white speaks of our joy,
  A home in God's kingdom for each girl and boy.

Traci Matt

Mocking in Moderne

Running Time: 2 minutes
Theme: Mocking of Jesus, even today
Suggested use: Maundy Thursday or Good Friday

They slinked around You
    those soldiers of Rome
    sneering spittle,
    their hearts as twisted as their whips.
If You were a king then they would worship You:
    swishing on a purple robe,
    ramming down a crown of thorns,
    forming its precious jewels with Your blood.
They slapped You with a stick,
    then posed it in Your hand like a scepter.
"You are our king," they said—
    a king of their own making.
And then the ultimate insult:
    they mocked You with false worship.
These were people You created, and Your heart broke.
But we, we would never mock You so.
Would we?
Do we?

We parade around You,
    we soldiers of faith
    sneaking profanity,
    our hearts as fickle as fog.

Since You are a King, we will say we worship You:
robing You in a numbered jersey,
plaiting a paper crown of money
that weighs like worry on the head.
We slap You with apathy,
take newspaper for Your book of law;
Then grant You a wireless mouse for Your orb
and a scepter of remote control.
"You are our King," we declare—
a king of our own making.
And then the ultimate insult:
we mock You with false worship.
Still, we are people You redeemed,
and Your heart breaks still.

Gail Blanton

Monologues & Short Scripts

Come to the Table

by Rob and Joanie Burnside

Cast:

JESUS
WOMEN—non-speaking roles

Props:

Baskets overflowing with fruits, vegetables, and baked goods
Crate or box
Linens
China
Silver pieces
Fine glassware

Setting: A bare table is set CS with two chairs. The table should be old, beaten, splintered, and obviously worn. Nearby is a crate/box that contains a linen tablecloth, napkins, china, fine silver, goblets, etc. Items need to be easily available, but hidden from the audience.

Production Note: This drama was performed for our annual women's retreat immediately prior to a communion service. The cast was all female and we used the same actress and costuming for the Jesus character for a short sketch at the beginning of the retreat.

JESUS: As this table is beaten and rough, so was the cross that I bore for you. Splintered and beaten was I, as I lay down my life and gave it up for yours.

(He pulls out tablecloth, unfolds it, spreads it over table, and sets remaining items out as the dialogue continues.)

Yet now, I clothe you in My righteousness and My sacrifice. Painful to watch and even more difficult to endure, it now undergirds the way for you to come and feast at the table. What once was ugly, unacceptable, and rejected by men, God has turned to use for unmatched bounty to all who will come and sup at My table. Come now, and join in the feast that My sacrifice has made possible. Know that I gave My all that you might enjoy His all—His table spread full of the blessings of life, life abundant.

(WOMEN *enter, walking through audience carrying baskets full to overflowing with items signifying God's abundant gifts to us. They proceed to the table as the communion service begins.)*

Matthew

by Dave Tippett

Cast:

MATTHEW

Costumes: Biblical dress

Production Note: This monologue can be used in conjunction with an established Easter-related choir musical/cantata, for example, or it may be used alone.

MATTHEW: Funny. I thought I was going to be able to leave my old life behind when I started following the Master. I have to admit that it is rather disconcerting to see people along the road who knew me as Levi, tax collector for the big "C" himself. "You!," they shout. "You cheated us out of house and home! What do you have to say for yourself?" At first, I used to try to keep them quiet, so the Master couldn't hear them. But I learned quickly that He knows much more than He lets on. And anyway, He's been to my house. He knows what I was.

It seems like only yesterday. There I sat, in my office. Doing business as I had always done it. Efficiently. I understood the people's hatred for me. Traitor, they would call me. Leach. But none of that mattered, for I was well paid . . . over and under the table.

On this particular day, it was quite hot, with dust in the air. As I sat and worked over my tally sheets, a shadow crossed in front of me. Annoyed, I looked up and there He was. Standing. Staring. I thought, "uh oh, another whiner looking to get more time for their payments." I was about to say something when He takes my writing tool from me, and lays it to the side. I couldn't believe the nerve! Words of protest were cut off as His eyes pierced mine and He said, "Follow me." For a moment I sat transfixed. Then I looked around me. Surely He was talking to someone else. "Who . . . ," then I remembered where I had seen Him. With the others. Those fishermen and the like. He was supposed to be someone special. A teacher . . . a rabbi with a heart for the poor. The poor. "He must know what I do to them," I thought. "Why would He . . . how could He even consider such a man as . . . I?" He stood there. Waiting for my answer. My eyes fell to different things around my office. The tools for calculating debt. The records and scrolls holding the financial information for hundreds. The scales. The money. And then . . . it all started to blur. In the wink of an eye, it all meant nothing. What was important five minutes ago . . . what was so crucial to protect and gather for Caesar . . . was now so much dust. My heart started to burn. A fire that I had never experienced. And, to my utter amazement, I slowly rose . . . removed my apron, and walked out of my life . . . forever.

He went with me to my home, where many of my friends . . . fellow tax collectors and others with less . . . noble professions . . . had gathered. He wanted to stay and eat with them. Them! The kind that others reviled. Rejected. He sat in their midst, spoke, and ate.

Of course, such news traveled fast and like dogs sensing an easy meal, the Pharisees arrived. "Why does this man eat with tax collectors and sinners?," they asked Jesus' men. All conversation stopped at once. Everyone looked at Jesus. He was the only one that looked unaffected by the Pharisees' charge.

I got up and was ready to make some sort of excuse when the Master went to the Pharisees and said, "It is not those who are healthy that need a doctor, but those who are sick. I have not come to call the righteous, but sinners."

There it was. The reason He had called me. I was the one who was sick. He hadn't asked me along because of my sterling attendance record at temple. I was the one who needed help, not all of those whom I treated so badly. The burning I had felt before was the start of the kind of healing only the Master could bring.

I gathered a few possessions and followed Him and the others out of town. I looked back at my home. I could tell that already my things were being divided up. But I didn't care. I was in the care of One who would provide all I needed.

And provide He has. To us. But to so many others too. Who were sick. Who were in need.

It's been a long while since someone has recognized me. Has hurled insults because of who I was. When it does happen, I simply apologize and explain the sickness I had . . . and how it was cured.

In a little while, we're gathering to eat together. To eat and laugh and reflect perhaps.

I wonder now, as I think back on that hot, dusty day when He came to my little office, if I hadn't stood up . . . and followed . . . would the diseases I had—the sin in my life—would it have completely overtaken me? I look at the Master now and thank God that I'll never know the answer to that question. I'll never know.

A Mother's Love

by Arlena Coffman

Running Time: Approximately 3 to 5 minutes

Synopsis: Two women share the grief of losing their sons

Cast:

WOMAN 1
WOMAN 2

Props:

3 chairs
Large bundle of clothes tied up

Costumes: Plain black clothes with dark shawls to be worn over head and/or shoulders

Setting: A quiet place, perhaps a park

(WOMAN 1 *is sitting in a chair on SL. She seems serene and in deep thought, a little sad.* WOMAN 2 *enters from SR, taking one of two chairs at CS. She is carrying—almost dragging—a large bundle, weary and sad. Sitting, she stares are the ground for a long time, then bursts into tears.* WOMAN 1, *seeing her tears, moves slowly toward her and sits in the chair beside her.* WOMAN 1 *watches for a moment, then reaches out and touches the hand of* WOMAN 2.)

WOMAN 1: Is there any way I can help?

WOMAN 2 *(startled, looks up)*: Oh, no. I just needed to find a quiet place to think awhile. I've just heard some bad news and had no place else to go.

WOMAN 1: I've found great comfort in this place. I've been coming here the past two days. It does help to sit and think. *(Starting to leave)* Perhaps you'd like to be alone, I just thought I could help.

WOMAN 2: Oh no, please don't leave! Perhaps you can be of help. You see, I'm so alone. I really don't know where to turn right now.

WOMAN 1: Do you live here?

WOMAN 2: No, I'm from the south. I only came here to find my son, but now, they tell me he is dead!

WOMAN 1: I'm sorry! I too am a stranger here and just lost my Son two days ago. I will be leaving with some friends in a few days, but meanwhile, I just have to go off by myself and think sometimes.

(Both WOMEN *look at each other, embrace, and softly cry for a moment.)*

WOMAN 1: It isn't easy losing a son. A son is special.

WOMAN 2: Yes, no matter what kind of son he is, there is no way to describe the loss one feels.

WOMAN 1: My Son was so good to me. I've just been sitting here thinking about our life together. There are so many memories, enough to help me through this. He would have wanted me to feel this way.

WOMAN 2: I have a lot of memories too. I try to only think of the good ones. My son was . . . different, I guess you could say. A little rebellious, like his father, but I tried to break it from him. He just had a mind of his own and was head-strong. But still, he was my son and I loved him dearly.

I remember him so well as a little boy, when he would gather flowers from the meadows and bring them home to me, his little face shining. I tried to raise him right, but I've asked myself a million times where I went wrong. So many people have advice, you know. You should have done this or not done that! I guess I tried them all, and still—maybe I was too lenient, or perhaps too strict. Does anyone ever know? I've cried so many nights wondering how I could have done differently. All I know is I did the best I possibly could for him. He finally broke away from me completely, running away at an early age. I spent many hours in fear of his life, until I heard he was safe. He seldom came home again and then, it was only a visit, never to stay.

WOMAN 1 *(throwing back her head in laughter):* Speaking of running away! I remember one time we had to go out of town, so a group of us traveled together. When it came time to leave, I thought my Son was with my husband, and he thought the boy was with me, but halfway home, we realized He was with neither of us! Imagine how we felt? I was so afraid. So we had to go back to get Him—a whole day's trip. I couldn't decide whether I was scared or mad at him. Do you know where we found Him? Sitting and talking to a bunch of old men, just as though nothing was wrong! I wouldn't even speak to Him on the way home, I was so angry. But He would just look at me and smile. We had a lot of laughs about it over the years.

WOMAN 2: Tell me, how did your son die?

WOMAN 1 *(a hint of bitterness):* He was murdered! A lot of people are saying it was just a misunderstanding, but I know better. And your son, what happened to him?

WOMAN 2: I'm not really sure. After my husband died a few weeks ago, I had no one to care for me, so I decided to try and find my son to see if he could help me. I had heard he was in this city, so I took what money I had and came here. I really didn't know where to start looking.

I went to the city officials and they knew him. It was there I learned he had died. There are so many conflicting stories I really don't know what to believe. It seems he may have been involved in something terrible. Some accusations were made . . . I really don't know what to believe. All I know is, he was my baby and I loved him. They took me to where he had stayed and let me take his things. He really had very few things, some articles of clothing (points to bundle), and some books. Then they did a strange thing. They gave me some coins they said were his. He had refused to accept them for some reason. I asked where my son was buried and they said he had no place. So I gave back the coins and asked that they buy a plot to lay him in. Now, I am without any money and I don't know what I'll do.

WOMAN 1: Please, *(rising)* come with me. I have people to help me. You can stay until you get yourself together.

WOMAN 2: But why would you do that? I am a stranger to you.

WOMAN 1 *(laughing)*: Oh, because you're alone and frightened, and because you are a mother like me, that is hurting. Come! *(Stretches out both hands to* WOMAN 2*)* And besides, I think Jesus would want it this way.

WOMAN 2 *(rising)*: Jesus?

WOMAN 1: Yes. He was my Son.

WOMAN 2: Jesus! *(Staring off)* What a lovely name! It sounds a lot like my son's name. *(She picks up bundle, clutching it to her.)* His name was *Judas!*

Alive

by Dave Tippett

Running Time: Approximately 3 minutes

Theme: Celebration of Christ's resurrection

Suggested Use: Easter Morning (Worship Service Opening)

Scripture Reference: Mark 16:1-13 NIV

Cast:

READER 1—Male
READER 2—Female
READER 3—Male

Setting: Sanctuary needs to be prepared ahead of time. On any windows with outside exposure, dark curtains need to be all the way down. Right before service begins, appropriate number of people need to be pre-placed at each window, but do not move until the end of the piece.

Production Note: Practice the timing of the slides carefully. There are times when things move along quickly, and the slide operator needs to make sure the flow is not interrupted.

READERS stand at SR, CS and SL respectfully. Each has their own folder and microphone. Each microphone should have some reverb.

Music may be played in the background of this piece. Production notes are provided to show when to bring the volume of the music up and down.

(At start, lights in sanctuary go down almost all the way. Dark, foreboding music starts to creep in. Slides of Jesus hanging on the cross fade in and out—and, hopefully, silencing the room. Last image is of Jesus hanging on the cross, and it remains as the piece starts, then fades away.)

READER 1: The end of the world.

READER 2: For us.

READER 3: All of us.

READER 1: All we had been through with Him.

READER 2: The healings.

(Slide **"Healing"** *fades in and out. Note—these slides fade in and out on each line, vs. waiting until line is delivered.)*

READER 3: The teachings.

*(Slide **"Teachings"** fades in and out)*

READER 1: The miracles.

*(Slide **"Miracles"** fades in and out)*

UNISON: The hope. The promises. All . . .

*(Slide **"Hope"** quickly fades in and out, **"Promises"** quickly fades in and out, **"New Life"** fades in and out-screen remains blank)*

READER 1: Gone.

READER 2: Gone.

READER 3: Gone.

READER 1: Doubt, darkness ruled our minds.

READER 2: Images of betrayal, beatings, death.

READER 3: Dreams of Him, only to awake to...

UNISON: Reality.

(Slide of empty cross fades in and out. READERS *stop, let moment linger, then dark music does a slow fade and goes out. After a few beats of silence, very faintly at first, then building is the simple SFX of birds chirping)*

READER 1: Until.

(Slide of a sunrise fades in)

READER 2 *(anxious):* Sir. Sir. What—what have you done with Him?

*(Slide **"Where is He?"** fades in and out-again, as line is delivered and not after)*

READER 1: Mary.

READER 2: Sir, I ask you again, where is He? Where is my Lord?

*(Slide **"Do you not see?"** fades on and out)*

READER 1: Mary.

READER 2: Sir, where is—

*(Slide **"Where is your faith?"** fades in and out)*

READER 1: Mary.

READER 2: If you have taken His body...

*(Slide **"Let not your heart be troubled"** fades in and out)*

READER 1: Mary.

READER 2 *(pause, then recognizing, whisper):* Teacher.

READER 1: Believe.

(Pause, more optimistic/hopeful music bed starts coming up)

READER 3 *(shouting, aside):* It's Mary! She's here. What is she so excited about?

(Music continues to build)

READER 1: What is it, Mary? You should not have come here. They are looking for us!

READER 2 *(out of breath):* I . . . I . . . have seen.

READER 1 & 3: Who? What?

READER 2: I have seen . . .

READER 1 & 3: Who? What!

READER 2: I have seen . . .

READER 1 & 3 *(increase volume / intensity):* Who! What?

READER 2: I have seen . . .

(Music reaches crescendo, then dies to silence)

READER 2 *(softly):* Him.

(Pause—SFX of a heart beat starts, and stays up, increasing in volume again, along with music bed)

READER 2: Alive.

(Slide of empty tomb fades in. At this point, the intro chords of an appropriate Praise and Worship song/hymn about Christ's resurrection starts-also, at this point, need to start cycling quickly the previous slides that say **"Healings," "Teachings," "Miracles," "Promises," "Hope," "Where is your faith?," "Let not your heart be troubled."** *Simultaneously,* READERS *continue, cascading their lines over each other.)*

READER 2: Him! Him!

READERS 1 & 3: He's alive?

READER 2: It's Him!

READERS 1 & 3: Alive?

READER 2: Alive!

READER 1: Do you not believe?

READER 2: Alive!

READER 3: Have you not seen?

READER 2: Alive!

(Slide cascading then stops and the word **"Alive"** *starts to grow as the last slide, fading in slowly as energy builds. Simultaneously, the helpers standing at the windows raise their respective shades to let in the light from the outside and the house lights start to come up at the same time.* READERS *still cascading over each other.)*

READERS 1 & 3: He's alive?

READER 2: It's Him!

READERS 1 & 3: Alive?

READER 2: Alive!

READER 1: Do you not believe?

READER 2: Alive!

READER 3: Have you not seen?

READER 2: Alive!

READER 1: Alive!

READER 2: Alive!

READER 3: Alive!

READER 1: Alive!

READER 2: Alive!

READER 3: Alive!

UNISON: Alive!

(At this point the Praise Team starts "Alive! Alive!" and READERS *step down and exit as the service continues.)*

Responsive Readings

A Responsive Reading for Palm Sunday

by Marty Parks

Scripture References: Exodus 15:2; Psalm 24:7-10, 118:16 NIV

LEADER: The LORD is my strength and my song.

CONGREGATION: He has become my salvation.

LEADER: The LORD's right hand is lifted high;

CONGREGATION: The LORD's right hand has done mighty things!

LEADER: Lift up your heads, O ye gates; and be lifted up you ancient doors.

CONGREGATION: That the King of glory may come in.

LEADER: Who is he, the King of glory?

CONGREGATION: The LORD Almighty—He is the King of glory!

A Responsive Reading for Lent & Good Friday

by Marty Parks

Scripture References: Romans 6:6; Galatians 2:20-21, 5:24, 6:14 NIV

LEADER: I have been crucified with Christ and I no longer live;

CONGREGATION: May I never boast except in the cross of the Lord Jesus Christ.

LEADER: The life I live in the body, I live by faith in the Son of God who loved me and gave himself for me.

CONGREGATION: May I never boast except in the cross of our Lord Jesus Christ.

LEADER: Those who belong to Christ Jesus have crucified the sinful nature;

CONGREGATION: May I never boast except in the cross of our Lord Jesus Christ.

LEADER: For we know that our old self was crucified with him so that the body of sin might be done away with;

EVERYONE: May I never boast except in the cross of our Lord Jesus Christ, through which the world has been crucified to me and I to the world.

Celebrate Easter: A Responsive Reading for Easter

by Gail Blanton

Scripture Reference: Psalm 107:2 NIV

LEADER: Jesus, our Lord, is risen!

CONGREGATION: He is risen indeed!

LEADER: "Let the redeemed of the Lord say so . . ."

CONGREGATION: Jesus, our Lord, is risen!

LEADER: Sound the shofar,

CONGREGATION: for the true Sabbath is here. *(Sound a shofar if you have one)*

LEADER: Blow the trumpet,

CONGREGATION: for this is the Lord's Day. *(Play trumpet fanfare)*

LEADER: Rejoice, all you instruments; lift your praise! *(All instruments play short intro into congregational song)* Sing, all you His people; lift your voices,

ALL: for we celebrate the day our Lord conquered death!

A Sweet Fragrance

by Gail Blanton

Running Time: One minute or less

Suggested Use: Easter Sunday

Scripture References: Matthew 26:12; John 12:3; Romans 6:4; 1 Corinthians 15:20; 2 Corinthians 2:14 NASB

LEADER: "Mary . . . took a pound of very costly perfume . . . and anointed the feet of Jesus"

CONGREGATION: Let us anoint our Lord with adoration.

LEADER: "and wiped His feet with her hair;"

CONGREGATION: Let us fall at His feet in confession and wash them with tears of repentance.

LEADER: "and the house was filled with the fragrance of the perfume."

CONGREGATION: Let us fill this house with the fragrance of praise.

LEADER: ". . . thanks be to God, who . . . manifests through us the sweet aroma of the knowledge of Him in every place."

CONGREGATION: Jesus said, ". . . when she poured this perfume upon My body, she did it to prepared Me for burial."

LEADER: ". . . we have been buried with Him through baptism into death."

CONGREGATION: "since we have been united with Him in His death, we will also be raised as He was."

LEADER: ". . . now Christ has been raised from the dead . . ."

CONGREGATION: Thanks be to God!

LEADER: On this Easter morning, when the earth is fresh with the sweet smell of new beginnings,

CONGREGATION: we, Your people, also come anew to celebrate and praise the sweet fragrance:

ALL: The fragrance of life!

Affirmations of God's Mercy and Grace

by Marty Parks

Running Time: One minute or less

Scripture References: Paraphrased from Psalms; Romans; 1 John; Revelation

Suggested Use: Lent

EVERYONE: The LORD is merciful and gracious, slow to anger and abounding in love . . . He does not deal with us according to our sins . . . for as the heavens are high above the earth, so great is His steadfast love toward those who fear Him; as far as the east is from the west, so far does He remove our transgressions from us.

LADIES: If we say we have no sin, we deceive ourselves, and the truth is not in us. If we confess our sins, He is faithful and just, and will forgive our sins and cleanse us from all unrighteousness.

MEN: If anyone does sin, we have an advocate with the Father, Jesus Christ the righteous; and He is the atoning sacrifice for our sins, and not for ours only, but also for the sins of the whole world.

EVERYONE: What shall we say to all this? If God is for us, who can be against us? To Him who loves us and has freed us from our sins by His blood, and has made us to be a kingdom and priests to serve His God and Father—to Him be glory and power forever and ever!

Service Openings

Opening Sentences for Worship: Lent

by Marty Parks

Sentence 1: We've gathered as the Body of Christ to remember His mighty act of redemption, to celebrate His presence among us and to offer our praise and thanksgiving to the One who loved us and freed us from our sins. Look now to the cross of Christ—a sign of sacrifice and of victory.

Sentence 2: Today is the first Sunday of Lent, a season of introspection, confession, repentance, and pardon. As we worship together, reflect on God's awesome presence, His loving redemption, His infinite mercy, His unbounded grace—and be thankful.

Opening Sentences for Worship: Palm Sunday

by Marty Parks

Sentence 1: Today is the beginning of Holy Week, seven days in which we commemorate Jesus' triumphant entry into Jerusalem and His atoning death on Calvary. From cries of "Hosanna!," which means save us now, to shouts of "Crucify!," our Lord displayed an unfailing love. Honor Him today with your sacrifice of praise—the fruit of lips that confess His name.

Opening Sentences for Worship: Easter

by Marty Parks

Sentence 1: Scripture records that God revealed himself to King Solomon, the prophet Isaiah, and the apostle John as a God of majesty, splendor, and holiness. Yet His desire is to draw all of us—the frail, the weak, the broken—to himself through His great love and through the sacrificial death of His Son, Jesus. Hallelujah! What a Savior!

Worship Service

Exalt the King

A Worship Service for Palm Sunday

by L. Ruth Carter

Songs: *Majesty*[1] / *All Hail the Power of Jesus' Name*[2]

Welcome and Opening Prayer:

Call to Worship: Zechariah 9:9

> "Rejoice! Rejoice!
> Rejoice with all your heart, O daughter of Zion!
> Shout aloud your praises, O daughter of Jerusalem!
> Look, your King is coming—he's coming to you.
> He is just and merciful, He is here to save you.
> He is humble, riding on a donkey, riding on a colt, the foal of a donkey.

Song: *Hosanna!*[3]

A Litany of Praise

Scripture References: Psalm 118:1, 14-29; Isaiah 62:10-11

LEADER: Oh, give thanks to the Lord, give thanks to the Lord our God, for He is good! His mercy endures forever.

WOMEN: Go through, go through the gates!

ALL: His mercy endures forever.

MEN: Prepare the way, prepare the way for the people.

ALL: His mercy endures forever.

WOMEN: Build up, build up the highway!

ALL: His mercy endures forever.

MEN: Lift a banner high, lift it up for all the people!

ALL: His mercy endures forever.

LEADER: For the Lord has proclaimed even to the ends of the earth:

WOMEN: "Say to the daughters of Zion,
'Look, see, your salvation is surely coming;
Look, see, His reward comes with Him,
Look, see, His work comes before Him.'"

Song: *All Hail King Jesus*[4]

LEADER: The Lord is my strength, the Lord is my song. He has become my salvation.

MEN: The voice of rejoicing and salvation is heard in the homes of the righteous;

WOMEN: The right hand of the Lord is mighty,

MEN: The right hand of the Lord is exalted;

ALL: The right hand of the Lord does valiantly.

WOMEN: I shall not die. I shall live and declare the works of the Lord.

MEN: The Lord has humbled, yes, He had rebuked me, but He hasn't handed me over to death.

LEADER: Open up the gates of righteousness for me. I will walk through them,

ALL: And I will praise the Lord.

Song: *How Majestic Is Your Name*[5]

LEADER: This is the gate of the Lord, the gate through which the righteous shall enter.

ALL: I will praise You, for You have answered me, and have become my salvation.

MEN: The stone the builders rejected has now become the chief cornerstone.

WOMEN: This is what the Lord has done. How marvelous it is to us!

ALL: This is the day the Lord has made; Let us rejoice and be glad in it.

LEADER: Save us now, O God, I pray. Grant us Your riches, Your blessing, for You want nothing but good for us.

ALL: Blessed is He who comes in the name of the Lord!

Song: *He Is Exalted*[6]

LEADER: The Lord, He is God. He has given us light. Bring the sacrifice to the altar.

WOMEN: O God, You are my God, and I will praise You;

MEN: O God, You are my God, and I will exalt You.

LEADER: Oh, give thanks to the Lord, for He is good!

ALL: For His mercy endures forever.

Song: *I Exalt Thee*[7]

Offering

Doxology

Anthem: *Shout to the Lord*[8] */ All Creatures of Our God and King*[9]

Sermon

Closing Hymn: *O Worship the King*[10]

---

[1]Jack Hayford

[2]E. Perronet, J. Eller

[3]Carl Tuttle or Michael W. Smith and Deborah D. Smith

[4]Dave Moody

[5]Michael W. Smith

[6]Twila Paris

[7]Pete Sanchez Jr.

[8]Darlene Zschech

[9]Mark Hayes

[10]Robert Grant and Johann M. Haydn